MAKING B

Making Blue

DIANA HENDRY

PETERLOO POETS

First published in 1995
by Peterloo Poets
2 Kelly Gardens, Calstock, Cornwall PL18 9SA, U.K.

A catalogue record for this book is available
from the British Library

ISBN 1-871471-50-8

Printed in Great Britain by
Latimer Trend & Company Ltd, Plymouth

ACKNOWLEDGEMENTS are due to the editors of the following journals and anthologies: *Ambit, Arvon Poetry Anthology 1985, Bananas, Critical Survey, Critical Quarterly, Encounter, Mandeville Press, New Poetry, Nonesuch* (University of Bristol), *Odyssey, Prospice, Peterloo Competition poster/leaflet 1994, Peterloo Preview 3, Poetry Book Society Anthology 3, Poetry Chicago, Poetry Dimensions Annual 5, Poetry Matters, Poetry Review, The Spectator, Writing Women.*

For Kate

Contents

page

Sunrise at Rethymnon

Maybe a plate, held half out of the sea's
sudsy bowl — yes, it is clean and gold enough —
or the big rim of an Olympian coin stuck
in the sky's slot. Almost you could push it
down in again, into the sea's dark box
and say 'Come back tomorrow'. The mountains

hunch under the shock of it. It is always
the same. They are never ready. Then it's
Rapunzel's braid, the gold rope tossed
down into the sea as if to rescue us or haul
us in. Why are we so slow learning how
to handle light? Why don't our hands evolve?

At least the church bells applaud. From
three corners of town and all out of sync
they jangle their uncombed rhythms, their
clappers still padded in sleep. And the ferry
from Athens — or a close hallucination — just
about makes its entrance. Only the birds,

showing off their formation dancing against
a back-drop of dithery t.v. aerials, aren't caught
on the hop. They sashay to the right again.
And oh, what a relief! The ferry has remembered
what to do. It is all coming back, like a dream.
It reaches the harbour wall and blows the day's

starter. 'Halooh! Halooh! Halooh!' it shouts,
terribly proud of its only line. The sun
slinks off, winching its gold flax up
behind it, closing the hatch. And 'Sky!'
we say, 'Sky!' Suddenly newly-made — or finished.

Making Blue

(for Hamish)

Here, in the harbour, the water is green.
Small fish needle themselves in and out
of its sheen, changing colour like wives
anxious to please a capricious spouse. Was
it fish taught the women how to embroider,
sitting, in black, in their doorways and dark
interiors, needles a tiny, fishy dash?

The nets of the fishermen are ochre and
bobbled with fat pink radishes. Picked
clean (by fingers stubborn as birds beaking
out worms) and spread on deck, here's a flash
jewelled cloak for the Merman King. How he'd
trail and boast it over his shoulder! How
richly the ruby radishes gleam! A giant's

baked sand-pies of concrete then tumbled
them out of his sack to fatten the quay.
The lighthouse, repro Venetian, explicitly
phallic, corkscrews its reflection back to
a notion someone once had concerning spirals.
Under the lighthouse, on its big stone doorstep,
a party of brightly-coloured tourists move

like cells on a microscope plate, afloat
in a fluid of sea and sky. Look — now
there's joining, now dividing. Over the water
you can hear them laughing, not knowing
what moves them, believing it's all their own
volition that pulls them into a cluster,
makes a trio, resolves it all in a final

couple, alone and hugging. The sea's trying
to find the far edge of sky. It's out there
somewhere, a roller towel with sea on one side,
sky on the other. When the sea has it measured
they'll go on their round together and
sky look up and sea look down. 'Till then
there's nothing else to do — except make blue.

The Arkadi Ferry

Four times a week, regularly, at the same hour,
it sails for Athens. How, when it boasts its departure
with three loud hoots, our spirits, even in sleep,
swell on the crest of it, are drawn as far after
as Antony by the fleet of Cleopatra's glances.
And even if you know all there is to know
of engineering and navigation, it is still miraculous,
such weight and bulk light on the water, its funnels
crouched like two black eagles, its mast a crucifix
held out before it. Pilot and tug boat scuttle
about it like miniature bridesmaids arranging
the waves and the winds. You think that the anchor
will never let go and when, at last, it goes grandly by
the harbour's eye, you want to applaud.

Four times a week, regularly, at the same hour,
it comes back like morning itself or the mother
whose faithful return you childishly doubted.
Is it the knowledge that one day she won't — or can't —
that gives to her arrival the profound relief
of the heart? And when she leaves again, is it
that you know she must, that it's life's imperative
and that for those we love we can only watch
and hope, standing on the quay and waving like mad,
dumbing the words that choke the throat? Over and
over it carries on, the journey out, the coming back
and the silliness of wanting it all to stop,
to be still, to stay forever and ever, though if
it did, we know we'd not know love at all.

Dimitri's Cherries

(for John Back)

The cherries Dimitri brings — a few, arranged
singly and brought on a small white plate —
are not like the cherries plumped and hyped-up
for market, heaps of them, lush and delicious,

lustred and glossy with money. Nor are they
the cherries that have travelled in trucks
down from wild mountains, still with the cold
of snow in their skins. These are quiet cherries

dark as communion wine, as the prick of blood
from the attic spinning wheel, as the small tight
bubs of a young girl's budding. Private, homely,
these cherries have that innocent garden look

as if someone, opening morning's shutters,
has said, 'The cherries are doing well this year'.
They go into my eyes and blood like a transfusion
these quiet cherries Dimitri quietly brings.

Song for the Sea of Crete

(for Anne and Henry Kernighan)

*"We are immersed in an enormous song and we shine like humble
pebbles as long as they remain immersed in the sea."*
— Kazantzakis

What matters is the sea — its saga
of light and wind and how it is faring
in its marriage with sky. Tonight
sky's drawn the line — will have nothing
to do with sea's incessant desire
to merge in a mist of dusky bliss. Sea
can stay outside and cool its heels.

What matters is the sea and how its master,
the sun, is treating it — beating its morning
metal until all the sparks fly, smelting it
into dimples and dazzles then nightly leaving it
solvent, soldered, sullen, steel.

What matters is the sea — how it hurriedly
flings down a rustle of satin it's forgotten
to iron; its sudden, revelatory blue
as you cut through a mountain
and it's down there heaving in its workshop
of passion, all frantic kerfuffle
and action, shaping waves in crescendoes,
honing a cut-throat phrase on a rock.

What matters is the sea: the ECT shock
and blue flash of its voltage; its hurl at land —
a child's leap at its father — its billioneth
dash; its rush in and out as for something
that's lost and of urgent importance.

What matters is the sea and the blue-
shadowed duvet it fluffs under the feet
of the tourist Icarus who float-flies over it
on a boat-drawn parachute. What matters
is sea's steady continuum beneath the beach bar's
fatal beat and the way when night at last rides off —
a girl in evening dress on the back of his *Vespa* —
sea just laps it all over as if nothing had happened.

What matters is the sea in the lull
of its harbour waters; its stormy tough stuff
beyond the quay; its beach fandango
in a can-can of petticoats. Mountains matter,
but only to say what the sea isn't.

What matters is the sea; its hunger
and hanker and danger; its hug and exposure;
its dedication to permanent change; its unpluggable
nature. What matters is the sea, the mass
and hugely blessed blue of it; its untranslatable
garbled message and the way it goes sailing out
to forever and ever and takes your heart with it.
What matters is the never-get-to-the-end-of-it sea

in its inky blacks and terrible deeps and how we,
like the lights on the fishermen's boats,
dance on the back of it, live on the edge of it,
breathe and dream and make up songs for it.
The sea. *Thalassa. Thalassa. Thalassa.*

The Lace Makers

(for Grace Brinkley)

They turn inward, to the dark of their doorways,
patient as porous rocks to soak up all shadow.
Only then, when they've bodily blotted up darkness
and each is as shadow-full as a fountain pen with ink,
can a few lines of White Mountain lace slip
like poesy's oozy gum, from their hooks and fingers.

The thread they use — drawn from a basketed spool
at their feet — might well be that which Theseus used
fumbling back from the gloom. Their crochet hooks
work like the mind making patterns of meaning. Their lace
they learnt as children watching foam and sea-spray
hem the beach. Now outside dark Venetian shops their cloths

dangle on poles and dazzle the tourists we've all become
with such a blinding white it's as if death itself
has been washed and sunned and the table laid for wine
and the bed for love and on each sheet and spread
there's lace to compensate for all that's rough on us,
that wounds the flesh with loss — of youth, or hope, or health.

Artemis, Still Hunting

From the back, promising. Hair: dark, curly (neither
too wild nor too tame and with endearing tendril centre
nape); froth of beard (Virile? Cheery?); specs; shapely
profile, shapelier knee. Colour sense is easy on the eye —
T-shirt an understated grey and shorts (well cut), dark blue.
Alone, a smoker and, god love us, reading a book! He has
the kind of cough it could be nice to wake to in the middle

of the night. I make all 'hello' noises known to man —
glass-clonk, lighter-click, unignorable see-how-much-we
have-in-common flutter of pages. Arrow-twang. Cough.
Nothing. The young Swiss boy, working at the baker's,
(starts at four a.m.) stops on his early way to bed
to chat about his day. The Greek at the table next
to mine asks what I'm reading. 'Po-et-ry', I say

spreading it out like 'Open Sesame'. What does it take
to turn a man's head? If a man hath all manner of promising
thing and shapely knee and hath not curiosity, he is
a soundless symbol. Curiosity takes me down to the corner
kiosk for a bottle of water, the saunter back contrived
to offer Chance the chance of a little soul-matery
or at least an up-front semiotic of another lone,

book-reading Being, wearing, I now see, my all-tame
bedroom slippers. Not that it matters. Heart-throb's
head down, hung-over, heart-broken — or both — over beer.
And anyway, the writing on his T-shirt's clear. 'Sprite',
it says. Just that. Ye gods, how was I to know?
He has a mortal cough. Drinks Amstel. Reads.

Sunbathing Song

I hate the sweat of it,
the grease of it,
the turning
as on a barbecue spit of it;
the roast, bake, fry and all the
peel of it;
the white-little-watch-strap-line and toasted
tits of it.

I hate the oil of it,
the boil of it,
the lying
flat on your back for hours and hours of it;
the sexless strip and the stingy dip you
mix with it;
the nine-to-five and the kiss-me-quix
you wear for it.

I hate the glare of it,
the bare of it,
the pubic
waxing bikinis need for it;
the sun when it's high in the sky
doesn't turn me on one bit;
I'd sooner siesta with Kosta in quest of
the hots of it.

I hate the melt of it,
the burnt pelt of it,
the sandy arse
and all the farce of it;
so leave this shady lady
laid in the shade,
baby,
for I love all of it.

October in Chania

It's the end of the season. The bawdy
springtime girl who sells wet sponges
on the corner of the harbour will soon be off
and the straw-hatted donkey who all summer
has clopped the round with tourists
in his trap, looks so weary, he could be Mary's.
Shutters are closing on tall thin houses.
Sun's over. Sea's restless as a fretful child.

October, and the beach taverna where we sit
with coffee, beer, wine and sandy feet
twined under the table, is almost empty.
The melancholy proprietor spreads out
his paper. He's going to make it last
all day, maybe tomorrow. He'll not look up
'till March. The tape deck's stuck on summer's
twanging lust for sun and sand and sex. In-

congruous lovers; connected only by lack
of connections, we're of our times. The light
here's such it would have Emily Dickinson
hearing the heft of funeral tunes. Is it now
our pasts rush in waving their papers
of remembered loves, accounts that list the losses
that freedom brings? An Englishman
at a corner table is watching us. The slogan
on his T-shirt reads 'No problem'. Is this
the moment when we know we're only transitory,

temps in love? When we hear the disappearing
whistle of the years, have intimations,
shiver in space? One step over the edge
and we could dive into oblivion or
our lives. Hold on tight to the world,
the table, your beer. Don't weep.
October won't last, but this moment will.

Piano Lessons

The terraced rows closed in and crushed you
in their jaws. At number ten, Miss Mildred
in her best front parlour, taught piano
on a neutered upright. All round
the walls were photographs of pupils who
had made the grade — past heroes of the
pianoforte, all capped and gowned and gone.
I found more promise in the piano's gold
and tabooed feet than in those haloed heads.

Somehow Miss Mildred smuggled in Beethoven,
fierce as sailors' rum. Quite drunk
on that illicit stuff, I'd pay my half-
a-crown and sidle from her spinster's den
prepared to find the neighbours risen
in outrage from their mothy beds.

In Defence of Pianos

(for Ben Kernighan)

In every alien place you find a piano —
schools, hospitals, prisons, asylums,
the homes of friends, your own front room.
Either they have been there forever
with a squeaky pedal and a dud B flat
or they breech-birth a window
and can't get back.

They should be extinct, these stranded uprights
lost in an iron-mongery moonlight
of genteel dust. The grand ones, got up
like mermaids in ebony velvet, bare
the awful symmetry of their jaws
in crocodile smiles
across the Albert Hall.

My Grös and Kallman, Berlin hausfrau, importantly
panelled and touched-up with brass, has two
timing pendulums engraved on her heart.
Her dreaming feet never touch the floor
and despite her homely Song-Book looks
she'll still flannel her hammers
with Wolfgang or Joseph.

O my frog-prince of furniture, I write
in your defence, having heard it said
that the lion's roar matches the desert,
the elephant's blare breaches the dark,
the bear can snarl at winter and snow
but man has only
a rented piano —

It is not widely known how far through the dark
of a night a piano can go, nor how
it can take to the streets in summer flight
so that hearing it ragging the silence you'd think
that man rented a forest to make a piano,
its falling pine needles
notes from home.

Solo

It is her music that I'll miss.
It's come to be her perfume in the house.
Rachmaninov's Second racketeering down the stairs
from the hi-fi gods of appassionata who live in her attic,
Brahms' *First* high romance and Elgar's cello
scraping the pelvic floor of grief.

She winters on the upright in the basement,
acquiring Mozart and Scarlatti
like a trainee sibyl, parsing rhythms
until the pitiless metronome gives in
to *The Rustle of Spring*. Then the cat runs
and *The Seasons* begin on the violin.

One summer it was all *The Moonlight*,
Christmas, Mozart's *Requiem*. On the journey
back from the Midlands, she lifted the roof off
the mini with hymns — 'O still small voice of calm'
sung indiscreetly loud. Hers was the alto part
in the choir. Queer intervals

From Poulenc's *Gloria* came from the bath,
senseless to us, until on the night
it all came clear, as might, perhaps,
the seasons of our lives, the full score
of us, heard from afar. Not
the still sad music Wordsworth knew
but more of Mozart in it, with the violins
frisking the shadows.

And then I fear false comfort —
but not as much
as the still small voice
and the silence filling up.

Teach Yourself Latin: Lesson Five

Adjectives. Class One.
Time When and Time How Long —
and there you are, beneath the Present's
blank transfer, a man in a garden
with a black cypress
and all your vocabulary growing around you:
leaf, garden, sadness,
lovely, loveliest bough,
always to look at,
to behold when full of shade.

Someone made you; uprooted a cypress out
of an ode and put you in a garden
and the first thing you open your mouth and do
is praise: 'the boughs and the leaves
of my black cypress dear to me are'
you say, your grammar not unnaturally confused
you not knowing where you are. Tempting

to try and follow you into the garden.
Your face is expectantly turned as though I had only
to come through the present
and you would describe the cypress against the sky.
Stay now, held where you are
between Time When and Time How Long
where the bough
of thy black cypress lovely, loveliest is.

Our Grendel

There must have been something else but sea.
I try to remember the school, the church, the people

but the sea was the real professional — the rest
an amateur production. However vast the cast

the sea went one better, put on an epic,
a clincher. No need to go and check its

credentials. Trading under a host of disguises
the parent company was easily recognised.

The council built a groyne, a wall, iron-railed
and then, in autumn, all else failing

sent for the sandbags. We lived, I suppose,
as the Geats with Grendel, our sandy homes

full of Chinese chests and shrunken skulls,
restless with women and empty of sons.

Grandfathers outside the pub with salt white hair
sat on in uniform and stared out there.

Soliloquy to a Belly

I have grown a belly.
It has swallowed up
my legs and arms,
even my head.

The government owns it.
Their man
comes to examine it
regularly,
like the meter.
I say 'I am behind it,'
but he has his union,
he has his schedule.

The old mothers
have come to my bedroom
to keep their vigil.
They sit and knit
strait-jackets for daughters.
It's the species that matter,
it's all quite natural;
little husk,
you're for corn.

Along the street
the no-bellies walk.
In the space between
their breasts and legs
they've a squeeze
of desire, like picnic salt
in a twist of paper.
They'd like a belly
to sleep behind.

I'm afraid
my arms and legs
won't grow again.
It happens every day of the week,
you're not unique,
not even special.

I'll hem my sheets,
I'll let them read the meter twice,
I'll be nice to the midwife,
push when I'm told.
I'm lying in
behind this belly,
thin and cold.

Great Grandma and James Andrew

It's not me they want in the photograph —
it's history they're after.
I'll not be part of it.
They can sit me on the sofa
and put the baby on my lap
and measure out, in black and white
almost a century's gap
between me, great grandma — eighty-four —
and James Andrew, newly born.

I can't refuse the pose. I can't refuse
the years. I can't refuse the law —
new life for old. But I won't smile.
I'll hold the baby, fold my hands
so he doesn't fall. When I stare
at the camera as I'm bid, I don't see
the birdie any more. Only the dark.

James Andrew turns his head aside.
The light from the garden has caught his eye.
He hasn't learned to pose and lie.
His fingers tickle. That child will be
the death of me.

No Garden to Speak of

What's left for you? All the past
has sieved through my fingers
and the family's so remarried or ruined
we've lost all connections. Somewhere
you are lined up with
Rob Roy MacGregor and a mad Aunt
Fanny who stayed in her room
for one whole year having lost
her soul — or so she said.

Even before we came here, half
the land that went with the house
had been sold off.
We've no garden to speak of,
and as for chattels —
plenty that's of sentimental value
but I scratch for a living,
for something of worth to see you through,
something constant that you
might open in the night and say 'Yes,
that is still true.'

Our ceremonies have shrunk to a candle
stuck in the head
of a Portuguese lady of two faces.
How close we all sit,
as if the rest of the house were taken
by soldiers. Keep the candle lit
and keep the tranquil space in the mind
that resembles a garden, a place
private but kind, where love might thrive.

Making Connections

Passengers talk through a porthole
to a man in a glass tank.
He has red-rimmed eyes
and a rubber stamp.

A scant metal bridge, humped
like the one on the Willow Pattern plate, spans
two platforms and a view
of the lost igloo city of cars
painted by children.

There's a photograph booth
(against loss of identity en route),
a news stand with *The Plain Truth*
available free, in a dark corner,
and a row of telephone cotes
to home in the lonely.

I eavesdrop the news —
'He should be here at twelve minutes past four'
(Twelve minutes past, repeated,
as if repetition will bring him for sure) —
and wait for her

who is too young to be running over bridges
after love and trains —
this little go-between, this bridge-hopper
moonlighting between mother and father.

Small as the Chinaman on the plate
she waddles across the bridge with her case.
'Why didn't you telephone me yesterday?' I scold
waving love's big stick.

The Stranger

1.

I help the midwife make the bed, a sheet
Of plastic first, to keep the mattress clean,
And then the draw-sheet, folded twice. I void
The thought of beds they dig by spade and fix
My mind on how to count the gaps between
The pains and when to push but still do not
Expect this gale force ten and you. Your head's
A bulb that's breaking through the self of me.

I see you crooked within your father's arm
As in a nest. One day I'll love you more
Than I can guess. Right now, resentful, tired,
Undone, I love and hate you all in one,
Reclaim myself and watch you from afar
And wonder — wonder who on earth you are.

2.

We quarrel while you're in the bath. I slap
Your face. You rise, an angry Venus from
The tub. My specs fly off, my hat is drowned.
I flash-back to that bath-time game when I
Played postman, you the giggling parcel bounced
Upon the postman's knees to Mrs Brown's.
(I played her, too). You lived out former lives
As apple, rose and lamb until un-towelled,

Re-born as you. Oh such a carry-on as you
Worked through the rites of growing-up. Today
I've trespassed and you've fled. I find a fall
Of undies on the floor like early selves
You've left. I bundle up your childhood years.
Out of their shell you step in self's new gear.

3.

I left you in your student room. You clutched
Old ted, lost all your teenage bluff and looked
Like ten again. The sturdy cabbie hired
To take me off, was well acquainted with
The autumn trade in freshly grieving Mums.
He had a spiel, Glaswegian, alien to
My English ear but though I missed a deal
Of what he said, he rolled his Rs about
Me like a rug and I took comfort from
His theory that the heart breaks only once

And breaking, breaks us in. But now I think
We're always leaving home and that the heart
Is slowly broken open all life through
By love or loss — as mine, by missing you.

4.

At least five times today we've almost met —
This morning in the shop; at a cafe down
The docks; your back disappearing round the block.
I saw your indicator flash its morse
Farewell and then we almost met again
As smiling you ran up to greet — someone
Behind me in our street. It seems you're not
The only girl in the world to look like you,
Though each who isn't makes me queasy, scared

That should you suddenly appear I might
Not know you. Queer, but I'm glad of ghosts and fear
That if they leave, I'll lose your shade to pin
Love to. Then love, that hall-light left all night
For you, might break its filament, or fuse.

Speaking Properly

(for Charles Tomlinson)

There can be no going back now
to my Russian gran
snapped in the back yard one summer
shy and untidy and still in her apron
as if a moment was all could be taken
from cooking and cleaning and washing for ten.
My great-gran's down in the basement
hid in her orthodox wig and her Yiddish.

As a child I thought theirs the exodus
after Moses, saw them coming like Cossacks
on husky-pulled sledges in icicled furs.
They were my romantic ancestors
who mortified my mum with their foreign ways,
their Vees and their Vyes and their Vobble-yous,
the X on the nationalisation papers
that listed the men and the children
but left out the wives. We turned

our backs on them, put up lace curtains
like the Berlin wall, went off to the shires
to learn to speak nicely and only later
felt their loss. I'd think of great-gran
home-sick for Riga, and heart-sick myself
for a *mama-loshen**, try to raise her ghost
and ask a few questions. She'd haunt
but not answer. Now, writing her off,
I understand why. She who'd had words
with Moses — Ai-yi-yi! — what had she to say
to me, born continents away, born yesterday.

mama-loshen ... mother tongue

33

Dressing Mother

I help roll her stockings over her feet,
then up to her knees. She's managed her dress
but I free her fingers from the sleeves.
Before the mirror she rouges her cheeks,
combs her thin curls, hands me a bow.
It's scarlet and goes on a ribbon I thread
under her collar and fix with a hook.
Over an hour to dress her today.

Such an innocence stays at the nape of the neck
it fumbles my fingers. I see her binding
bands of scarlet at the ends of my plaits
and fastening the buttons at my back.
Now look — she's dressed as a child off
to some party. I straighten her scarlet bow

and don't want her to go,
don't want her to go.

Portrait of a Gent

Yes, there is something of you there —
idealised, of course, but a passing
likeness. A mistake, perhaps, to turn
that scarlet bath towel that you wore
into a toga. And that dream I draped
so becomingly over your left shoulder —
well, a nice idea, but awfully dated.
I've given too much lustre to your
hair, straightened your nose (though
its crookedness was more endearing)
and made of that vulnerable look of yours
something far too immortal. Oh, everything's
there, that's there, but somehow distorted.
I've touched you up, so to speak,
yet missed an essential sweetness.
As for the expression in the eyes —
is that yours or mine? For though
the whole struggle of the artist
is to be clear-sighted, there's so much —
as in love — that blurs the heart;
fictions, the self, the past. Well,
here you are, or someone like you.
Reserve judgement. Be kind. That
dark and passionate background is lovely
don't you think? And did anyone ever see you
in such an exquisite light?

William Herbert, Chancellor of Oxford University, 1617—1630

Here stands William Herbert cast in bronze.
His smile declares that he was much approved
by God. And all that he believed and stood
for once, is yet corroborated here
by fold and scroll of stone, by towers that still
aspire, by colleges that last, by large
and leisurely-rivered parks and by this quad
where Reason and its Chancellor stand on.

What was it like, I want to ask, to swell
your chest, to curl your whiskers, have no doubts?
To see the world spread all its secrets out?
Bronze-hardened father, he'd not answer that.
'It was' he'd say, 'because' he'd say. We pose
for photographs; he debonair with hand
on hip, aloft his everlasting plinth
and I inept, equivocal, unwrought.

Norman MacCaig's Heart

So many poems
have passed through it
it must be as sweet and clean
inside
as a cider press
when apples have been.

The Builder's House

This was Mills the builder's house:
outhouse after outhouse
at the back, as if from the start
he was travelling out. The kitchen,
a shack at the side, had a stove and cold tap.
There were buckets to catch the leaks
from the roof, walls unpainted, rooms
unheated — the whole place neglected.

A life-time he spent doing the houses
of others, his own left undone
but for one refinement — in every
dark cupboard he fixed a light.
And maybe he had his priorities right —
leaving the front of his life unpainted
and all the dark places light.

Settling Down

She has been working at it sixteen years,
kindling grievances, bolting doors,
allowing flesh to mount like unwashed dishes
on her boards. In her linen cupboard

neatly-folded, moth-balled doubts rise
in piles. She's never shed a thought
but keeps them layered in a flower-press
of wrongs, the screws turned tight.

Each new idea's as deftly spiked
as a bill upon a nail. She's laid up
logs of prejudice, burnt, in bundles,
love that might have kept her warm.

In the cutlery compartments of her mind
fire and water never mix.
Her life's twitched straight, the hectic
sheets are smoothed, the bed is made.

Mental Patients in Peace Time

No war can excuse them,
the plebeian mad
with their clichéd Christ dreams,
untended hems and marriages
imitatively bad.

Stunned by some lock on the brain
that sometimes twists,
they stare at mince and mash
on plates too thick
for cutting wrists;

or follow the trolley
that trafficks the wards,
that flies a brave nurse,
that plies clip-board cures,
that rattles a curse.

Manics blow in
in galleons of generous smiles —
here's to the electric cat,
here's to Greek chorus girls!

They say this is a villa
in Wild Country Lane —
tell us its name.
Sacrifice,
damnation,
spendthrift waste
would give us status:
we are the unseasonably mad —
only relate us.

Home-made Angels

He was right, the prophet in the park
saying, 'The balloons are coming tonight!'
For here they are — rising up over the city
like a hallelujah! Rising up
over house, church, office block, to appear
en masse in the sky as angels might
only gorgeous and gaudy and saucily transcendent,
uttering the message in a sudden rush, a roar of fire
HOSANNA IN THE HIGHEST. THIS IS US!

Each dangles a picnic basket of people,
little puffed-up souls sailing the skies
as if they'd just discovered immortality to be
easy as riding a bike or walking the sea.
They make the night Arabian,
are a sign in the sky from us to us, as if,
earthbound, we exhaled belief
as naturally as breath and dreamt them up,
these flights of fancy, our rough guess.

Funeral Dance

The spire is as perfectly centred
as the black and white priest in the doorway's arch.
Left of centre stands a large yew.
Six staunch bearers pace the path.
On the raw oak box, the shields of flowers
are heraldic crests that mock
our claims. Outside the gates
the mourners make two half moons.

Bach could have set it as a four-part fugue
but for the shapeless figures
in sullen grey who stumble, unsynchronised
after the coffin, breaking the dance,
draining the colour out of the grass,
making the priest seem sawdust and silk,
neutralising spire, yew tree, arch.

Outings

1. SUNDAY AFTERNOON DRIVE

Held in work-silent poise all week
and now set tolling. The bells
of the mind ring their mad changes until
like beaten translators we fling up our lives:
drive out.

A landscape of moors and stone walls is on
the screen. Wind's in stereo.
On the reservoir cute toy sails
bob like Miss Olive's ballerinas,
battery born.

We drive as we sleep and die, separate
yet side by side: choose
the beaten track or the unknown moor,
gag or claw, death-in-the-middle
keeps the score.

2. FOR THE TOURISTS

As to an evangelist they're drawn
to Bolton Abbey. Strays
in unsuitable shoes climb hills, uncertain
what they're looking for. Tea shops open up
like whores.

Grassington turns out its trinkets.
At York they say it costs
a pound a minute to maintain the Minster.
Would you buy two minutes of Christian
history now?

In the lounge of Harrogate's Royal Baths
a dressed-up lady tells
an audience of unsoiled children
how the Alhambra fountains ran with the blood
of thirty-six princes.

3. SIGN-POSTS

In the Sunday drone of an empty town
three stones caged in iron,
incised by cup and ring. These faint
statements still the bells: from the distance
the authentic calls.

Bored with the armistice of views
the children sleep. We drive.
You have the wheel, I the guide.
A tractor's bridal train of gulls
is tossed by wind.

In Peril in Venice

(for Rachel Edwards)

Carried off like Leda
on a British Airways swan
and landed somewhere on the Lido
feeling deathly as Donne
in his hymn about shipwreck.

Madonnas, madonnas everywhere
hold out their arms to Venetians
and victims of the plague but stare
indifferently at tourists
such as me, and the only message

in the skies is the neon 'Campari'
on the closed casino. Dark nights
are not a part of our itinerary — though
an upset stomach is all right
and disorientation's expected.

I suffer from neither.
It's not the lack of a map
and the language that makes me blub —
it's Mary's lost lap
and St Christopher's shoulder.

The Homely Pigeon

'Is it a pigeon?' I kept asking
the way one asks
is this the man I married
and what has possessed him
rushing in through the French windows
in grey gothic cloak
like a Shakespeare messenger?

Not the dove, swooping into the ark
of the moneyed apartment,
nor the quick light flight
of Bede's bird through the hall.
This bird's fat and urban
and full of interrogating silence.

Is he the one?
The shy boy at the party
fingering his tie
now grown bold and daring
a cold gloat in his eye

disturbing.
Why did I not see
the artificial colouring of his breast
and beneath his shirt-tail
the appalling nail-lacquer pink
of his wrinkled legs
and loose-skinned claws?

I hold out bread
which he ignores.
He has no tidings
only a tag
ringed round his claw
in broken English,
the identity bangle
that tells his faith:

I am homely
I am homely
I am homely.

Glasgow Sparrows

(for Kate and Scott)

It's two or three in the morning —
too early, surely, for the dawn chorus,
unless the birds of Glasgow, hearing of their city's
rise in cultural glory, want in on the act.

The bed, borrowed from my daughter,
is in the heights of a decayed Greek mansion —
domes, pillars, mosaics — below, a hall
where the post of a vanished generation

overflows a side-board. Today we tramped
a large and hairy mongrel in the park.
They take themselves seriously, the buildings
of Glasgow; start all solid sandstone pomp then

peter out sillily in spindles of gothic frills
and quivers. Perhaps its these, translated
into sound, I'm hearing now. Such trills
and transcendence as must be nightingale.

I'm not surprised: neither grace nor thunderbolt
arrive when expected. Somewhere I've read
the date when nightingales last were heard
in Berkeley Square. Are these from there?

Delayed, perhaps, by the century's weather.
Outside, in a van, my daughter sleeps in the arms
of her man under nightingales in Glasgow trees.
Is it all in the listening? Before,

mere twitterings? This song's somehow known
yet new. I memorise the first four notes and then go
blissfully wrong. By ten o'clock my daughter's
at the door with milk and Sunday paper.

Dog bounds in after, all fret and fever.
'I heard a nightingale last night,' I say.
'Sparrows,' she says, 'confused by street lights.'
She puts the milk away. I settle for sparrows,

reviews of Larkin's letters and the dog.
You could comb happiness like static in his coat.

Skylark Research

I am the skylark researcher.
I am keening my ears for them,
eyeing people in the street,
asking 'Do you believe in skylarks?'

Nobody has seen one.
They look at me as if I've spoken
an exiled word.
I worry that skylarks have been expelled,
become dissident birds.

I try to pretend they are simply out
of fashion, like Shelley,
but secretly I'm afraid
they have been hushed up,
or that something has happened to our hearing,
or that the hinge has broken on heaven's gate
and there's nothing to sing at,
or that they've worn themselves to a frazzle
singing their hearts out
at the blank sky.

Perhaps there's a change in our climate.
Perhaps the fluttering of cash cards
keeps them silent.
Perhaps they can't be heard above the din
of Help lines ringing through the night.

Possibly it is not yet dark enough
to set them off
and they are up there, arrowed
and waiting to wing from the bow.

Sometimes I imagine
a mass dawn vigil
and skylarks rising
up over the inner cities,
lifting the low skies
of England.

I romanticize.
I have nothing uplifting to say.
I am here to record
the comings and goings of the common lark.
I keep the word fresh for them.

I am the skylark researcher.
Bulletins fly from my fingers.
I airmail the news.
It is my job to report
on what is beyond reach,
out of sight,
not spoken about,

there.

All Hail the Hollyhocks

Freaks, flapping their leaves
like albatross wings when
to be discreet they should lean
against some husbanding wall,
pose prettily beside a door.

Exposed and unsupported
these show-offs flaunt their flowers
in public. Neat, low clumps
of things mumble at their feet,
the clingers and grippers,
the rooters and spreaders
who talk of decorum.

The hussies ignore them, intent
on the terrible toil of growing,
the doubtful strength,
the engorged bud,
the threat of snail slime, rust and slug
and the shame
of being too tall, too much,
too altogether hollyhock.

Well, now they're wind instruments
flowering at every stop.
They're summer's gothic,
they're hitting the high spots,
they're shooting their mouths off
hysterical to have made it
past the clothes-line
past the first floor windows.

Gangling, tranced teenagers with earphones on,
they're humming sun and sky,
beyond everything,
shaking with laughter.
Tomorrow they'll flash another flower or two

they're going straight through.

Pollarding

There is no correct age for pollarding
trees and dreams. Ideally
one should wait until the girth
is five to seven inches,
the dream just filling out.

The first cut may be made some six
feet up. If the dreamer's
not allowed to go too far
a short ladder may be
used to bring him down.

Side shoots ought to be removed
or else they turn into
new dreams. It's a winter job,
December is ideal.
Don't let a dream see spring.

To protect cut-ends and hopes from rot
a fungicide should be used,
but a quick wipe-over with old diesel oil
or a bit of real life
is cheaper and just as effective.

Sycamore Seeds

Airy as hopes the sycamore seeds
have blown into my garden.
Their skeleton propellers lie
in the grass like the abandoned
transport of refugees fleeing
the tree two gardens down.

A population explosion has taken
over my twelve-by-twelve
urban patch. If I let them grow,
we'll be back to forest in under
three years: Wodwos return;
snakes sigh in the grass.

My neighbour says no other tree
has as strong a grasp on earth
as the sycamore. You must root
out seedlings fast. Left
too late, you'll have to use poison.

There are sycamore trees
in my mother's garden. They've
outstripped the house, eaten
her light. It's sycamores, not
the meek, who'll inherit the earth.

Fetching a knife I think, 'best
befriend the rarer species — waste
can't matter for this common lot.'
Yet drawing their thin, striving
roots out of soil, I'm sad

not to give them a chance —
these hopefuls pushing the just-
published shoot of themselves up
into green; these tentative
beginnings, these might-have-beens.

Underwear

Knowing a new lover
means new knickers,
I escalate to *Lingerie*
where passion's pastel,
lust is muted
and the body most genteelly neutered.
Not a nipple to be seen
and the plastic girls all shaved clean.

There's rails and rails of fantasy pants,
hip-huggers, high-leggers,
half-garter, bikini —
Oh much has changed
since I was last
on a quest for knickers
in which someone might see me.

Here's all the tit and tat of tease,
narcisstic soft porn, silky sleaze.
How could I dream of his hands hot on
my spotty, worn out, M & S cotton?

And why should I
with my not un-notched bed-post
feel so shy?
I clutch my coat close
and button my dress up to my throat,
for fear a candid camera's eye
should see right through
and find me shocking
-ly dressed
in flesh and desire.

Rescue Attempts

Sometimes I think about rescue
And wish that rescue would come —
Though with age I've almost forgotten
What I want to be rescued from.

Was it from a life like mother's
Or from a perch on the shelf?
Was it from an endless marriage
Or was it from myself?

Whose hand held out the rescue —
Was it God, or Love or Fame?
And why did the charging Chargers
All look much the same?

It was never to do with arrival,
It was all to do with the flight
When like a Dulac illustration
I flew through Arabian Nights.

When I heard the bridegroom coming
I put on my clothes and left,
Crying like St Augustine,
'Not yet! Not yet! Not yet!'

Which makes me doubt my desire
Is anything like sincere,
And that if I'm not very careful,
I might prefer to be here.

So why does the thought still linger
As doom comes inexorably slow
Of a crane that drops a grab of love
When there's only seconds to go?

Compleynt

Pity the girl who's one of a trio —
she has to do everything with brio.

Would the Little Mermaid have danced upon knives
if God hadn't invented wives?

An immortal soul is poor compensation
for a here-and-now relation.

Understanding the passion of life
is not as comfortable as playing wife

and there are times when a cup of tea
is better far than ecstasy.

The eternal triangle has sharp edges
and many Ms's are left on ledges.

But a trio, perhaps, is less monotonous
than us than us than us than us.

Safety Pins

A precaution against things falling apart;
a metal metaphor connecting affinities
and contrarieties; a way of fixing
a note to a pillow, a heart
to a sleeve; useful for making
a makeshift attachment; a yoke or appro-
priate betrothal symbol; a child's

first brooch, clipped to the hips; an early
buckler; upholder of hope and knickers; a boon
to heroines undone and nuns so in love
with the Lord they desire
to be pinned to his bosom; an improvisation on
the common theme of loss of buttons
and beloveds; a magic token given third sons
by the witch of the wood to run the risk

of social occasions; a piece of silver
to solder the self, to fasten clasp and snap
shut all uncoupled couplings; used, in armies,
by dry cleaners keeping clothes in PC order;
an instant hook to stop time flying,
tea-towels fleeing; a homely staple; staple
item; nose-ring; nurse-tag; better than a stitch;

than nothing; a cautionary tale
on the dangers of safety; the unclinching nature
of body and soul; the propensity of love to fray.

Small Hours

('*Lord, you made the night too long*' — Louis Armstrong)

Are the long ones; when no-one phones,
when the fridge drones, when yesterday,
held to a match, shrivels to nothing
and tomorrow, unmapped, stretches to nowhere.

Unlived lives shiver in the small hours,
prison looms, love shrinks,
fear shakes out its samples of shadows
and asks you to choose. Hope unspools.

In the small hours the last light
goes out, stars are doused,
the heart's lost, the moon never was,
the silence shouts. The small hours

are the long ones, when everyone's gone
and darkness ticks on and on and on.

The Body's Vest

Often I wish a thief would steal it,
or a tutting mechanic thumbs-down it,
or the police clamp it, or the Lord,
lowering a crane from the sky, up-reel it.

Each morning it waits to claim me,
demands oil and water, somewhere to go
and a hand to steer it. I confess I fear its
love of journeys; its Homeric glows shame me.

Others go by who put their lives on
every morning and sit inside them
and seem at home and know the way —
perhaps I've the wrong shape and size on?

Often I think I'd like to leave it,
an abandoned creature on the verge,
and 'casting the body's vest aside'
slip off on a slip-road and never retrieve it.

Two Christmas Poems

ON THE CHRISTMAS LIST

Like evolution the Christmas card list,
no dramatic change, just the drop
of a name or a change of places,
a slight acquaintance upped to friend,
a cast-off aunt or mother-in-law's
ex-lover tippexed to rest.
It's the survival of the fittest,
of those whose warmth outlasts
a year or two or three then sifts
the heart's strata from limestone
to silence. I knit the geology
of love, add three, slip two — each
Christmas it's the same, a list of names
like thoughts for a christening.

CHRISTMAS

is never where you expect it.
Not in the big house
with the fire lit and the presents rustling,
nor when the lights awaken
the tree and you should feel something
and don't.
Christmas happens in an unimaginable
place — in a city store with canned music —
in the street with a stranger
and a white cyclamen,
or when the silence tightens
the cry in your throat.

Then Christmas comes,
never where you expect it
and always in Bethlehem.

A Love-charm

Three words I'm walking round.
I hold them to the light,
expose them to the dark,
watch them like cakes in the oven,
to see if they're ready,
put them under the scan
to be sure they've quickened,
lay their letters out
to check for sense and spelling.
Test their toxics,
try them on spit and spindle,
send them off on the big dipper,
define their chemical components,
make seventy percent proof;
spin in a gyrostat,
shake the dust out of them,
plump up, flesh out,
tongue thin, worry at,
peg on the line,
starch, bleach, clean,
send sadly back.

They will not do to tell
What the body says so well.

Prayer for Rain

Lord, you who can make
the Australian desert flower
with a single rainfall
once in seventy years

remember me, whose
three score years and ten
are running out.